Welsh Country Cookery

Traditional Recipes from the Country Kitchens of Wales

BOBBY FREEMAN

Contents

First impression: March 1988
Fourth impression: March 1990
Fifth impression: July 1992

© Bobby Freeman 1988

ISBN: 0 86243 133 6

Photographs of the John Thomas Collection
(courtesy of the National Library of Wales).

Printed and published in Wales by
Y Lolfa Cyf., Talybont, Dyfed SY24 5HE;
Talybont (097086) 304.

Note on American conversions

*It is not always possible to accurately convert
British to U.S. Measurements—we have been as
careful as possible with these conversions, but as
precision is not an important factor in Welsh
cookery, any slight discrepancies which may occur
should not have an adverse effect upon the
finished dish . . . if in doubt use your own
judgement.*

Dolwyddelan castle, one of Owain Glwyndwr's strongholds

INTRODUCTION

It's easy to assume (and the assumption is all too often made) that traditional Welsh food is nothing more than thin broth and oatcakes, enlivened perhaps by the odd Welshcake off the bakestone, or a slice of curranty *bara brith*.

There is plenty of evidence to testify that this was largely the day-to-day diet of the rural poor in Wales for long periods when times were particularly hard—one of them occurring late enough to affect living memory; which is why this view is so often allowed to prevail.

The depressed period of the early years of this century is bitterly remembered; its terrible monotony smothered any latent sense of enjoyment in food—as something for experimentation, or for the entertainment or discussion—rather than something simply to fill the belly as quickly as possible at minimum cost. I am sorry to say that even in these days of comparative affluence there is still a general unwillingness to pay for quality in food and drink: there is, nevertheless, a growing, not to say *rapidly* growing, market throughout Wales for fine quality, locally-produced foods, free from additives and organically-grown and reared.

Monotonous they may have been, but the old foods were healthy enough: oat dishes, wholemeal bread, buttermilk, home-cured bacon, the warm, filling potato dishes: all are remembered with great fondness by older folk. A woman now in her seventies tells of her upbringing on an enlightened farm in mid Wales, where food was never short. Her mother won 1st prizes for her butter, they kept up to 500 hens and her father grew vegetables in careful rotation. Neighbouring farms were not always so well managed: lack of attention to hygiene and dairy bacteriology led to rancid and unsaleable butter, for example.

She was taught to cook over the 'fire on the floor', manipulating the heavy iron 'crane' to adjust the height of the iron pot or cauldron suspended from it over the flames. She remembers the big weekly baking-day (Friday) when the wall-oven was heated: "bread in the morning, then cakes and tarts when the bread was out, finally large tins of rice pudding with currants or raisins baked in the cooling oven for 2-3 hours, or left overnight".

But her mother remembered the terrible poverty when the farmers had to sell all their eggs—only the cracked ones were available for the family. Butter then was only used for cakes at Christmas and weddings, at other times it would be bacon fat or other dripping. Most of the cookery books, she says, were for the big country mansions where a lot of staff were kept … "Simple recipes written on odd bits of paper were invented and circulated by housewives using whatever ingredients they had to hand."

Her grandfather was fond of the old barley bread and often had a few loaves specially baked for him. It went stale very quickly but was good while still fresh. When the weekly bake of bread became stale in hot weather, the loaves were dipped in milk a short while, then re-baked to freshen them. She remembers tremendous sessions of fruit-bottling and jam-making, and their dependence upon stores of root vegetables.

Her most joyful memory is of the day her mother acquired an oil stove: "I was able to mix up a Victoria sponge or little cakes in the middle of the week!"

Having once tried to make apple dumplings as a young wife, and had them fall apart disastrously in the cooking, I can appreciate the skill required to make them in the *cawl*! As a summertime treat, the dumplings were thrown into the boiling *cawl* about an hour before the midday meal, "served at noon, prompt—we had to be very careful to seal them well for if they opened up in the *cawl* the menfolk would soon tell us—and even refuse their basinful of *cawl*,"

the same woman remembers. When done, the dumplings floated on the surface and were ladled out and kept warm.

This 3-course dinner was cooked in the one pot for economy's sake. First came the broth, then the meat and vegetables (from the *cawl*), finally the dumplings, served with brown sugar and milk or cream.

'Kettle broth' must surely epitomise the depths of poverty—when all a mother could give her children before sending them to bed warmed, and their hunger a little comforted, was a hot mash of boiling water poured over broken bread crusts and sprinkled with pepper and salt. A similar dish in Wales was called '*cawl dŵr*' (water broth). Old people still enjoy it when down with a heavy cold, or 'flu: "Boil an onion until thoroughly cooked, in ¾ pint of water, then add 2 teaspoons oatmeal made into a paste with a little water, boil this for 5 mins, pour into a basin, break some pieces of bread into it, add a lump of butter, pepper and salt and a pinch of ground ginger—then off to a warm bed."

The year 1935 must have marked the end of the old ways with food on the farms in Wales, when the Milk Marketing Board collected their milk in churns and they gave up butter and cheese-making which were thenceforth bought in weekly.

Greater educational opportunities, more affluence and foreign travel have encouraged a widening of culinary horizons to a hitherto unimaginable degree for today's up and coming generations in Wales. Indian, Chinese, wholefood and vegetarian cookery are being enthusiastically dipped into today—as is, alas, the microwave for 'junk food'—a far cry indeed from the old iron cauldron hanging above the open fire, or the *ffwrn fach* (pot oven) set on its tripod over glowing coals.

Nevertheless, I have to admit that the quickest and best *caws pobi* (roasted cheese) is made in seconds in the microwave; while old hands with the famous, almost national dish of Wales, the meaty, chunky, root vegetable and leek broth the Welsh call '*cawl*' have discovered, as is only natural, the labour-saving way of preparing it for the pot in the food-processor. . .

Many of the old Welsh dishes still have their place in everyday Welsh life (my young neighbour, for example, would not dream of making her Welshcakes other than on the bakestone, albeit over her modern gas cooker) and are often delicious in their simplicity. A cookery of the people evolves naturally, as with the food-processor *cawl* and microwave *caws pobi*—and one other I know of: *siencyn*, the early breakfast of bread and butter with hot tea poured over

. . . now a busy housewife leaves it ready with a teabag atop the bread and butter ready for the early riser to pour on the boiling water.

The simple fare of most parts of rural Wales is not the whole answer to the Welsh culinary scene of the past. Well-to-do farming families in the richer, lowland areas always fared better, and there one does find more of a sense of relish for richer dishes and fine wines. This was often in the tradition of early English cookery as it developed from medieval cookery, as practised in the great houses of the Welsh nobility, itself descended from Norman-French, which in its turn was more or less a return to Britain of the cookery of the Romans. Here and there in all Welsh recipe collections there are contributions evident of a cook skilled above average, trained perhaps in the kitchens of a great house. In the old counties of Montgomeryshire and Radnorshire, along the border with England, there is a strong tradition of elegant cookery, bearing witness to the influence of the many mansions in the area. One of my favourite MS recipe books is that of Merryell Williames of Ystumcolwyn Farm, Meifod, Powys, a clear record of late 17th century cookery practised in a prosperous farm household by an accomplished cook and treasured housewife, as her husband's tribute on her gravestone suggests: 'a prudent, virtuous and tender wife'.

SPRING

Pastai Cennin
LEEK PASTY

Simple and good—a useful accompaniment or snack.

	I	M	A
shortcrust	8 oz	225g	1 cup

2 or 3 medium-sized leeks, white
and best green parts
4 rashers fat streaky bacon

Line a baking plate with half the pastry, cover with finely-chopped washed leeks. Lay strips of bacon on top, season, add an egg-cup of water, then cover with the remaining pastry. Make slits in the top, paint with beaten egg, bake in a hot oven (400°F, 200°C, Gas 6) for ½ to ¾hr. Serve hot. You can add a few herbs to the filling if liked, or enrich it with a couple of beaten eggs.

Cawl Cennin
LEEK SOUP

lb peeled potatoes
1 lb leeks (incl. the *tender* green)
3 pints (75 fl. ozs; 7½ cups) water or chicken stock
1 dsp. salt

Exact quantities are not important and this soup is a splendid base for the addition of left-over or fresh vegetables. Moreover: if you use chicken stock, increase the seasoning and stir in up to ½ pint cream when it is cool, before finally chilling it, *cawl cennin* asserts its French connection and lo! *Vichyssoise!*

Slice or dice the potatoes, slice the leeks thinly, simmer together 40-50 mins. (or pressure-cook—but don't microwave). Mash the vegetables or liquidise. Check seasoning and re-heat—or chill.

Crempog Las
GREEN PANCAKE

	I	M	A
flour	½ lb	225g	1½ cups
2 eggs			
spring onions or shallots			
chopped parsley			
milk to mix, approx	½ pt	275 mls	1¼ cups
pepper and salt			

Make a batter with the flour, eggs and milk—
much stiffer than for ordinary pancakes as it
must be able to support the onions. Chop these
finely and add, with the parsley and seasoning.
Cook gently on both sides over a very moderate
heat in a heavy frying pan. Make sure they are
cooked right through. Spread with butter and
serve hot as an alternative to potatoes or bread
with meat or bacon, or with cheese, as a snack

Crempog Hufen
CREAM PANCAKES

Pancakes are still, as of old, delightfully popular
in Wales: a treat, especially for birthdays. Apart
from the fact that they were considered best
made with buttermilk and bicarbonate of soda
(see Lightcakes) instead of sweet milk, the
universal basic pancake mixture is used.

Cream pancakes, however, are a special luxury, and recipes for them can be found in almost
every Welsh mansion's MS recipe book. This one
is from Slebech Hall in Pembrokeshire (use
pullets' eggs or reduce to 6—eggs, like people,
were smaller 200 years ago):

**'Mix together 2 large spoonfuls of flour, a pint of
thick cream, 4 whole eggs and 4 yolks and fry in
the usual manner '**

Cawl
BROTH

Ah, but *cawl* in this sense means more than just 'broth'. Whereas at one time it was divided, in that the broth was drunk first, and the meat and vegetables eaten second, the way the French do with their *pot au feu*, which *cawl* closely resembles (except that it is actually a better dish), today it is taken all together in a companiable bowl. A wooden bowl if possible, and a wooden *cawl* spoon, hand-carved, so you won't burn your mouth on the hot broth. With a hunk of wholemeal bread and a chunk of good cheese there's nothing better on a cold winter's day. It is now readily available, in pubs and restaurants with a Welsh atmosphere, in the tourist areas of Wales. Exact quantities are not important:

for 2 lb weight of meat (bacon or lamb with a smaller piece of brisket or shin of beef), 2 large parsnips, 3 large carrots, 1 small swede turnip, 2 medium onions, 2 or 3 leeks and 1½ lbs potatoes (tiny, new potatoes are best).

This amount will need a large pan and will serve up to 8 people, but *cawl* is best made in a large quantity—it can be reheated or frozen for future use.

Brown the meats first to give a good colour to the broth, then cover with cold water and bring to a simmer. Skim, simmer about an hour, then add the vegetables, roughly cut. Leave the potatoes till later if they are small and new. Flavour with plenty of thyme or winter savoury, parsley, bayleaf and one or two cloves—and I like to add celery. Season with whole black peppercorns, leaving the salt until later. Some Welsh cooks thicken the *cawl* with a handful of oatmeal or flour and water paste. Add some of the leeks towards the end of cooking time, but leave the rest to slice very fine and sprinkle on the top of each bowl with lots of fresh, chopped parsley as you serve, so they stay crisp, crunchy and peppery.

Pastai Persli
PARSLEY PIE

Shortcrust pastry
2 eggs
2 rashers bacon
1 dsp. flour
2 tbls. sugar
1 dsp. chopped parsley
½ pt (275 mls; 1¼ cups) milk
little bacon fat

I'm inclined to think that the sugar in the custardy filling of this little pie is a carry-over from the old days when it went into savoury dishes as a matter of course. Line a deep pie dish with the pastry. Mix the flour with a little of the milk, beat the eggs with the rest and add to the blended milk and flour with the salt, sugar and parsley. Lay the bacon cut in small dice, on the pastry, pour in the custard, bake in a fairly hot oven 30 mins. or until it is nicely set and is cooked through. Leeks can be used in place of parsley. (400°F, Gas 5, 205°C)

Tatws Llaeth
POTATOES WITH BUTTERMILK

A simple dish, well-loved in timed past, and still by older folk when they can obtain real buttermilk, which is thin and yellowish—with the increase in on-farm butter-making this is not as difficult to get as it was a few years ago. From the Spanish cook who worked for me and who came from the Celtic area of northern Spain I learned that the same dish was just as popular amongst country people there. The only difference was that they beat the potatoes to a mash with a fork.

Boil potatoes (new for preference) in their jackets, peel off the skins and serve in individual bowls. Pour buttermilk over and eat while warm.

Oen Cymreig Melog
HONEYED WELSH LAMB

	I	M	A
Welsh lamb (leg or shoulder)	3-4 lbs	1½ kilos	3-4 lbs
cider	½ pint	275 mls	1¼ cups
Welsh honey	½ lb	225g	½ lb
2 tbls. rosemary	1 teas. ginger	salt & pepper	

This is not, I think, traditional, but it is very
good. Rub the joint (NB Welsh Lamb is smaller
than other breeds and the meat sweeter) with
salt, pepper and ginger, leave ½ hour to absorb.
Double-line an ovenproof dish with foil, place
the joint on it, spread honey over the meat,
sprinkle with rosemary. Pour cider all round.
Roast 30 mins. in a hot oven, then lower heat to
moderate for a further hour. Cover the joint if
you wish for the first half of the cooking time,
otherwise baste at intervals, adding more cider if
necessary—at all costs avoid allowing the honey
to catch.

Ffowlyn Cymreig
WELSH CHICKEN

	I	M	A
1 chicken			
bacon	½ lb	225g	½ lb
carrots	½ lb	225g	½ lb
2 large leeks			
a small cabbage			
stock	½ pt	275 mls	1¼ cups
butter			
bouquet garni	pepper & salt	*beurre manié*	

The Welsh *ffowlyn* suggests a boiling fowl, and
the recipe derives from a very old one. Truss the
fowl. Cut the bacon and carrots into small
pieces, fry in butter until just brown. Put the
bird on the top of this in a heavy pan, together
with the leeks, herbs and seasoning, pour in the
stock, dot the bird with butter, cover and simmer 2-3 hours (less for a roasting chicken). Cook
the cabbage separately and make a bed of it on
which to serve the chicken, surrounded by its
vegetables. Boil up the stock, thicken with 1 oz
flour worked with 1 oz butter (*beurre manié*) and
added in little pieces—pour around the chicken
or serve separately.

Teisennau Cocos
COCKLE CAKES

Prepared cockles are mixed in a thick batter and fried, a spoonful at a time, in hot fat.

Another traditional way with cockles is to fry them in bacon fat and then pour beaten eggs into the pan, stirring well with a wooden spoon to create what is, in effect, scrambled eggs and cockles. Season with plenty of fresh-ground black pepper. This dish was thought to be an aphrodisiac.

Cocos Pen-clawdd
COCKLES PEN-CLAWDD

prepared cockles
fresh breadcrumbs (white or brown)
spring onions
butter   parsley
salt and fresh-ground black pepper

Exact quantities don't matter for this dish, which comes from the shore-side village in north Gower where both laver and cockles are processed. Melt some butter in a heavy pan and throw in breadcrumbs and finely-chopped spring onions. Stir these about until the butter is absorbed and the crumbs become crispy, then add the well-washed cockles, pepper and salt. Then—'clap a lid on tight for they cockles do jump!', shaking the pan vigorously over the heat to make sure the cockles are quickly heated through. Sprinkle generously with chopped parsley and serve.

Migiod
YEAST BUNS

	I	M	A
wheatmeal flour	1½ lbs	675g	1½ lbs
molasses sugar	3 ozs	75g	3 tbls.
butter	2 ozs	50g	½ stick
currants & sultanas	2 ozs	50g	⅓rd cup
milk (approx)	½ pint	275mls	1¼ cups
candied peel	1 oz	25g	1 tbls.

1 egg   pinch salt   1½ teas. dried yeast

These buns are traditional to Pembrokeshire (part of the New Year celebrations in the past). They are best eaten warm, and I think they are improved by using 85% brown flour instead of white.

Rub the butter into the warmed flour. Beat the egg into the warmed milk, stir dry ingredients into the flour. Froth the yeast in a little warm milk, then add to the milk and egg and pour into a well in the flour, mix well and knead. Prove for 1 hour in a warm place. Cut into 18 rounds, place well apart on a greased baking sheet, prove again until double in size. Bake in a hot oven 15-20 mins. Brush with melted honey to glaze.

Bara Carawe
CARAWAY SEED BREAD

	I	M	A
wheatmeal flour	10 oz	275g	2 cups
rolled oats	2 oz	5g	¾ cup
bacon fat or veg. oil	1 tsb	15 mls	1 tbls
tepid water	½ pint	275mls	1¼ cups
molasses sugar or honey	2 oz	5g	2 ozs
salt	1 teas	5 mls	1 teas
caraway seed	1 teas	5 mls	1 teas

1 sachet easy-blend yeast

Add the salt, sugar, seed, and yeast to the warmed flour and oats, make a centre well and pour in the oil and water. Mix to a dough. Knead well on a floured board, then set to rise for about an hour in a warm place. Knock back, shape into a shallow 2pt greased loaf tin, make a cut down the centre, sprinkle the top with oats, bake about 40 mins in a mod. oven (370°F, 190°C, Gas 4) when the top should be a lovely golden brown. A nice sweet bread for tea and an unusual accompaniment for a mature cheese.

Bara Brith
FRUIT LOAF

	I	M	A
wheatmeal flour	1 lb	450g	1 lb
yeast (dried)	1 teas.		
molasses sugar	2 ozs	50g	2 tbls.
butter	3 ozs	75g	⅔ stick
milk	¼ pt	150mls	⅔rd cup
seedless raisins	3 ozs	75g	½ cup
currants	3 ozs	75g	½ cup
candied peel	1 oz	25g	1 oz

1 teas. salt   1 teas. mixed spice

The famous speckled (with fruit) bread of Wales, best made as originally with brown flour and yeast. Add the spice to the flour and make as for bread, cutting the butter up and melting in the warmed milk for the dough. Work the sugar and fruit into the dough at the second kneading. Bake in a 3 pt. loaf tin 20-30 mins. in a hot oven (425°F, Gas 7, 220°C), covering the top with paper for the final 10 mins. Leave to cool a little before turning out. Brush top with sugar syrup to glaze. (The butter and sugar can be increased if a richer cake is preferred.)

Ffest y Cybydd
THE MISER'S FEAST

mealy potatoes
slices of bacon or ham
onion
salt and pepper

This was originally an expedient for getting two meals out of one—the potatoes mashed in the nourishing liquor one day, the bacon with a fresh boiling of potatoes the next . . . hence the name. The idea is similar to that of 2-day *cawl*. It comes from the days of the iron-pot suspended over a fire.

There is something innately satisfying about the combination of bacon and potatoes, especially when they are nice and mealy as they should be for this. Cover the bottom of a heavy pan with whole, peeled potatoes and a sliced onion. Cover with water and a little salt and pepper, and a lid: bring to the boil. Now put the ham and bacon slices on top and simmer slowly until the potatoes are cooked through and most of the water absorbed.

Pwdin Caws
CHEESE PUDDING

4 thick slices crustless bread
8ozs grated cheddar cheese (225g; 2½ cups)
1 pint milk (575mls; 2½ cups)
1 egg   butter
cayenne pepper   nutmeg

An interesting development of *caws pobi*, perhaps. . .at any rate an unusual supper or lunch dish when accompanied by a crisp salad.

Toast the bread on one side, butter the other side. Place 2 slices, toasted side down, on the bottom of a greased ovenproof dish. Spread half the cheese over the beaten egg, season, repeat. Boil the milk, add seasonings and beaten egg. Pour over the pudding, leave to soak at least ½ hour. Bake in a mod. oven (350°F; Gas 4; 180°C) until risen and pale gold on top. Serve at once (2-4 people).

Teisen Sinamon
CINNAMON CAKE

	I	M	A
flour	8 ozs	225g	1³/₅ cups
sugar	4 ozs	125g	½ cup
butter	4 ozs	125g	1 stick

2 egg yolks
2 egg whites
½ teas. baking powder
1 teas. cinnamon
milk to mix   apricot or raspberry jam

This unusual cake is so improved by just the addition of one extra egg yolk and one (or perhaps 2) whites that I cannot resist giving my own version. The contrast between dark cake and white topping is most appealing.

Rub the butter into the flour and baking powder. Add the spice and sugar, then the yolks and a little milk to bind to a fairly stiff sponge. Turn into a shallow, well-greased tin or plate. Bake in a hot oven (400°F, Gas 6, 200°C) for about 20 mins. Cool and spread with jam. Make a meringue topping with the egg whites and 1 tbls. caster sugar per white. Return to a cooler oven (325°F, Gas 3, 170°C) to set and until the peaks are tipped with gold.

Teisennau ar y maen
BAKESTONE CAKES

	I	M	A
flour	1 lb	450g	2½ cups
butter	6 ozs	175g	1 cup

cooked apple, rhubarb or other fruit
brown molasses sugar
butter

It took me a long time to learn to make these scrumptious treats successfully (by the way, you don't need a real bakestone—a heavy frying pan will do) until I found they could be made in rounds, rather than folded over like Cornish pasties. Make up the pastry, cut into 4-5in rounds. Drain the cooked fruit really well, place on a round, damp the edges and cover with another round, pinching the edges tightly together. Cook gently on both sides on a moderate bakestone until mottles with gold. Now comes the *pièce de resistance:* trim the edges of the rounds and ease the lid off with a sharp knife. Work sugar and butter into the hot fruit, close the lid, serve at once with whipped cream.

Leicecs
LIGHTCAKES

	I	M	A
flour	4 ozs	125g	scant cup
sugar	3 ozs	75g	3 tbls.

¼ teas. bicarb. soda
1 egg   pinch salt
milk, or buttermilk to mix

These are best made with buttermilk—a Welsh cook told me that *all* Welsh drop-scones and pan-cakes are best made with buttermilk and bicarbonate of soda. Lightcakes should be small—3-4ins across.

Mix the dry ingredients in a bowl, but if using buttermilk, dissolve the bicarb. in this, then beat up with the egg. Pour this mixture into a well in the centre of the flour etc. and beat to a thick, creamy batter. Drop in spoonfuls on to a hot, well-greased bakestone or griddle. Turn when bubbles appear on the top surface and the underside is golden. Serve warm with butter.

Cacennau Iago
JAMES' CAKES

	I	M	A
flour	6 ozs	175g	gen. cup
butter (softened)	4 ozs	125g	1 stick
sugar	2 ozs	50g	2 tbls.

These little, thin, shortbread 'cakes', marked with a scallop shell, were made at Aberffraw on the west coast of Anglesey and are often called 'Berffro cakes' instead of their correct name which reflects the pilgrims' scallop shell motif for the shrine of St James in Northern Spain.

Work the sugar, flour and softened butter together, using warm hands, to make a paste which can be rolled out thinly and stamped into rounds with a plain cutter. Mark each round with a scallop shell if you have one. Instead of following the original instructions to bake quickly in a fast oven, I bake mine for up to ¾ hr. in a slow oven (300°F, Gas 2, 150°C) until they are faintly coloured and crisp.

Slapan Dafydd
DAVID'S BATTER CAKE
An Anglesey recipe

	I	M	A
plain flour	10 ozs	275g	2 cups
butter	2 ozs	50g	½ stick
sugar	3 ozs	75g	3 ozs
sultanas	3 ozs	75g	3 tbls
buttermilk	½ pint	275 mls	1¼ cups
2 eggs			
1 tbls. wine vinegar			
1 teas. bicarbonate soda			
½ teas. salt			

Put the flour, salt and sultanas in a bowl. Melt the butter in the buttermilk, then gradually pour into the dry ingredients. Beat well. Leave to stand a few hours if possible. Beat the eggs, add sugar, soda and vinegar, then pour into the batter, beating well. Pour on to a moderately hot greased griddle to make one large cake. Turn when golden on the under side. Split in half while warm and spread with butter to serve.

Teisen Ffwrdd â Hi
QUICK-MIX CAKE

	I	M	A
plain flour	8 ozs	225g	1¼ cups
butter	2 ozs	50g	½ stick
sugar	2 ozs	50g	2 tbls.
currants	2 ozs	50g	⅓ cup
pinch salt milk to mix			

This is a griddle, or bakestone cake, which is meant to be split while still warm and spread with butter to serve.

Rub the butter into the flour, add the other dry ingredients. Mix with milk to a stiffish mixture which will spread evenly over a moderately hot, well-greased bakestone or griddle. Bake on both sides until golden.

Gwin Blodyn Eithin
GORSE WINE

	I	M	A
gorse flowers	3 pints	1.7 litres	3 pints
sugar	2 ½ lbs	1¼ kilos	2½ lbs
water	1 gallon	4.5 litres	20 cups
yeast + nutrient			

This is a simple recipe, given to me by a Pembrokeshire woman—you may wish to add oranges and lemons and grape tannin as in newer recipes. I have not yet made this, but keep promising myself I will, for James Williams wrote so glowingly of its virtues in *'Give me Yesterday'*.

Pour the boiling water over the gorse blooms, leave to steep for a week. Strain, heat the liquor to tepid, then add the sugar, and when dissolved and cooled, add the yeast, leave to ferment for a few days and then put into jars fitted with an airlock. It may need racking-off after a few months before the final bottling. Ready in about 8 weeks.

Gwin Dant y Llew
DANDELION WINE

	I	M	A
dandelion flowers	4 pints	2 litres	10 cups
sugar	3 lbs	1.5 kilo	3 lbs
water	1 gallon	4.5 litres	1 gallon
2 lemons 2 oranges (juice and rind)			
yeast + nutrient: ½ oz			

One thing, there are always plenty of dandelion flowers. Made in April (the flowers should be gathered on St George's Day, April 23rd, or at any rate, at noon, when they are full and dry) it will be ready for Christmas. Discard as much green as possible from the flowers but don't worry too much about this. Pour boiling water over them, cover with a thick cloth, leave 2 days, no more. Strain. Add sugar, boil 30 mins. When cool, add the yeast, put into fermentation jars, fit air lock and rack when cleared. A little citric acid added to the finished wine will deal with the odd taste which may develop as the wine matures.

SUMMER

Selsigen Morgannwg
GLAMORGAN SAUSAGES

	I	M	A
white or brown breadcrumbs	5 ozs	150g	1¾ cups
hard cheese, grated	3 ozs	75g	⅓ cup
butter	1 oz	25g	¼ stick
1 small onion			
1 egg			
pinch dry mustard	pinch mixed herbs		
coating crumbs			

These are much nicer than you might suppose, freeze well and are popular with vegetarians. Eat them with a sharp, spicy sauce, like tomato.

Mince or chop the onion very fine and soften in the butter before adding to the other dry ingredients—this makes shaping the sausages easier. Separate the egg and bind the mixture with the yolk. Divide into 6 small sausage shapes, moulding with your hands, then roll in flour, dip into the lightly beaten egg white, finally roll in fine, toasted breadcrumbs. Deep fry in hot oil until the coating is nice and crisp.

Brithyll a Chig Moch
TROUT WITH BACON

1 trout per person
thin rashers streaky bacon
lemon and parsley stuffing
salt and pepper

The idea of wrapping a trout around with thin rashers of streaky bacon is a good one, as the fat lubricates the fish and the combination of flavours is not unhappy. If you also add a lemon and parsley breadcrumb stuffing you have something very special.

Use brown trout if you can, otherwise the ubiquitous rainbow trout. Clean and gut the fish, remove the backbone, and stuff. Use the bacon rashers as binding to hold in the stuffing, then lay the fish in a greased baking dish and bake 15-20 mins in a mod. oven. The bacon on top of the fish should be just lightly crisp.

23

Eog Teifi
TEIFI SALMON

Often presented as 'Teifi Salmon Sauce', this recipe illustrates the 18th century passion for using butter as a cooking medium—thus it is not a sauce at all. Nowadays we would reject its dangerous cholesterol level in dismay! The original recipe probably came from one of the Teifi valley's many mansions:

¾ of a pint of melted butter, together with a glass of port, a little ketchup (probably mushroom) and one small boned anchovy were used to bake a whole fish—a relatively small one I would think. Try baking a whole salmon, or a good tail-end, *dotted* with butter and with the other ingredients poured over, covered with foil, in a med. oven for 30-40 mins. Pour off the juices, add the port and ketchup, boil up and serve as a sauce to the baked fish.

Tarten Llugaeron
CRANBERRY TART

	I	M	A
cranberries	1 lb	450g	1 lb
raisins	½ lb	225g	1 cup
sugar	1 oz	25g	1 tbls.
rich shortcrust	10 ozs	275g	10 ozs
vanilla essence	½ teas.		

Tiny versions of their cultivated American cousins, cranberries grow wild in upland Wales, underneath other plants on wet, boggy land. This recipe is from Radnorshire—as I have not come across a reference elsewhere it is reasonable to assume that only in that area were the berries accessible from habitations.

Put the first 3 ingredients in a basin and leave overnight. Turn into a saucepan, bring slowly to a simmer, hold for 5 mins. Add vanilla; cool. Make a plate tart with the fruit and pastry, bake in a hot oven (425°F, Gas 7, 220°C) about 30 mins. Eat hot or cold, but *always with cheese*.

*Pice ar y maen**
WELSHCAKES

	I	M	A
SR Flour	8 ozs	225g	1¼ cups
butter	4 ozs	125g	1 stick
currants	3 ozs	75g	½ cup

1 large egg
½ teas. baking powder
pinch nutmeg or mixed spice
milk to mix

These are traditionally made on the bakestone (griddle) and are best eaten while still warm. Some mixtures give a dry, biscuity result—this one is richer. Rub the butter into the spiced flour, add sugar and currants, bind with beaten egg and a little milk to make a stiffish paste. Roll out on a floured board to about ¼in. thick, cut into 2in. rounds and bake on a greased, moderately hot bakestone 3-5 mins. each side until mottled golden brown. Sprinkle with sugar.

* lit. 'cakes on the stone'

Teisen Afalau Surion Bach
CRAB CAKE

	I	M	A
SR flour	1 lb	450g	3 cups
caster sugar	6 ozs	175g	scant cup
2 large eggs			
pinch salt nutmeg			
butter	4 ozs	125g	1 stick

It is the jelly from the crab-apple which gives this bakestone cake its name, and the recipe comes from the Vale of Glamorgan, one of the few areas in Wales where crab-apples grow. Rub the butter into the flour, add sugar, salt and nutmeg. Make into a stiff dough with the beaten egg, roll out into two plate-size rounds. Spread one with crab-apple jelly, cover and seal edges tightly. Bake both sides on a moderate bakestone—a large wooden paddle is useful for turning it.

Jeli Mintys Gwsberen
GOOSEBERRY MINT JELLY

2 lbs green gooseberries
good hunch of fresh mint
sugar

A most useful addition to the store cupboard—as an accompaniment it gives a good Welsh air to simple roast lamb. Put the berries (no need to top and tail) in a large pan and just cover with cold water; cook till soft. Strain, and to each pint of liquid add 1 lb sugar. Put in the mint, tied up in a bundle (about 6 large stalks), heat gently until the sugar is melted, then boil for a jell. Remove the mint, pour into glass jars and seal. The preserve has a pretty pink colour.

Bara Can
LUXURY LOAF

	I	M	A
white bread flour	1 lb	450g	1 lb
butter	1 oz	25g	¼ stick
warm milk (approx)	7 fl ozs	200mls	1½ cups
1 teas. dried yeast			
2 teas. salt 1 egg			

Some years ago, the *'Sunday Times'* asked me to adapt the old Welsh bread recipes to the present day for their book on Real Bread. Subsequently, I produced my own little book 'Welsh Bread'. This, and all the other bread recipes are taken from this work. *Bara Can* just means 'white bread', but as it was a 'special occasion' loaf I called it 'Sunday Bread'. It is rich and satisfying, with a thin, crisp crust.

Dissolve the yeast in a little warm milk. Rub the butter into the flour, add the beaten egg to the yeast with the milk, pour into a well in the flour and knead to a nice, shiny, dough. Shape into one large loaf, set to rise in the tin 1½ hours and bake ½ hour in a hot oven, then reduce heat to mod. for 15 mins more.

Cwstard Tywysog Cymru
PRINCE OF WALES' CREAM

	I	M	A
milk	1½ pts.	30 fl ozs	3¾ cups
sugar	8 ozs	225g	1 cup
gelatine	½ oz	12g	1 teas
3 eggs			
2 lemons			

Which Prince of Wales? Not Llewelyn or Glyn Dwr—they're too early for this recipe, and Charles is too late. It's typical of the many little lemon desserts of Victorian times, so it must be Edward. The custard will curdle if the milk is too hot for the eggs, and the same risk applies if the mixture is not really cool before the lemon juice is added. Dissolve the gelatine in the milk. Add the sugar and the thin peel of the lemon. Boil for 5 mins. Cool, gently insert the eggs, well beaten. When almost cold, add the lemon juice and strain into one mould or individual glasses.

Pwdin Mynwy
MONMOUTH PUDDING

	I	M	A
white breadcrumbs	8 ozs	225g	3 cups
milk	½ pt	275 mls	1¼ cups
granulated sugar	2 tbls.		
butter	2 tbls.		
2 egg whites			
nutmeg red jam or fruit			

Many old puddings bear the name of a town, but the historic old county town of Monmouth (now in Gwent) seems to have been the only Welsh town with this distinction.

Boil the milk, pour over the crumbs, cover and leave 10 mins. Break up with a fork, work in the butter, sugar, nutmeg, and finally the stiffly-beaten egg whites. Put a layer of jam or fruit on the bottom of a greased glass soufflé dish, then a layer of crumb mixture. Repeat until the dish is full. Bake, covered, for about 30 mins. in a very mod. oven (350°F, Gas 4, 180°C). You can cover the top liberally with brown or white sugar and caramalise under a hot grill. Serve slightly warm with plenty of cream.

Teisen Mêl a Sinsir
HONEY & GINGER CAKE

	I	M	A
plain flour	1 lb	450g	3 cups
butter	4 ozs	125g	1 stick
sultanas	3 ozs	75g	½ cup
glacé cherries	3 ozs	75g	⅜ cup
runny honey	8 ozs	225g	½ lb

a little candied peel
2 large teas. baking powder
2 large teas. ground ginger
2 eggs   milk to mix   pinch salt

A rich, old cake from the time before sugar was cheap. Honey is a moisturiser so it will keep well in an airtight tin.

Melt the butter gently, add honey & a little milk. Cool. Sift flour, salt and b.p. together, add dried fruits. Add the beaten eggs to the honey and butter mixture, and then to the dry ingredients. Mix thoroughly, with more milk if necessary. Bake in a greased baking tin in a moderate oven (350°F, Gas 4, 180°C) 1-1½ hours.

Teisen Carawe
SEED CAKE

	I	M	A
plain flour	1 lb	450g	3 cups
butter	8 ozs	225g	2 sticks
caster sugar	5 ozs	200g	5 tbls.
caraway seeds	½ oz	10g	1 tbls.

2 eggs   2 teas. baking powder

The oldest and most enduring of our egg-raised cakes (caraway seeds offering small challenge to the eggs as early cooks experimented without yeast) and still liked by older people in Wales today with its associations with chapel and Sunday tea in the parlour.

Sieve flour and baking powder. Rub in the butter, add the sugar. Beat the eggs with a little water and mix all together—a fairly stiff mixture. Bake 1-1½ hrs. in a mod. oven (350° F, Gas 6, 180°C)

Bara Ceirch
OATCAKES

4 tbls. medium oatmeal
½ tbls. bacon fat, or oil
3 tbls. hot water

Welsh oatcakes were traditionally made very large, huge in comparison to those of Ireland and Scotland—as big as dinner plates. They were baked on one side only, then stood up against the fire to harden the other side. They required great skill to manipulate by hand into the large, thin rounds. The small quantities given here are explained by the advisability of mixing and making just a few oatcakes at a time. There are fatless recipes, but this is the one I prefer. It is important to use medium grade oatmeal.

Heat the fat in the water, sprinkle the oatmeal on to it, kneading well. Flour a board with oatmeal, form the dough into small balls and roll out thinly (as big as you can manage!). Bake 5-10 mins. on a moderate bakestone or griddle.

Sopas
JUNKET

	I	M	A
milk	1 pint	575 mls	2½ cups
caster sugar	1 teas.		
rennet	1 dstp. or junket tablet		

There is for me something appealingly refreshing about the combination of junket and oatcakes for breakfast on a warm summer's morning. Junket was fashionable when I was a child in the 1930's; after a long time out of favour it is slowly returning in today's climate of healthy eating. It was certainly enjoyed on the farms in Wales in the past.

If you buy junket tablets or powder the instructions for making will be on the packet; either way the method is the same: warm the milk to blood heat (98.4°F, 35°C) in fact its natural heat, put it in a bowl or deep dish in which it will be served, add the sugar and stir in the tablet or rennet. Leave in a warmish place until set, then chill well before serving.

31

siencyn te: sometimes called 'the shepherd's first breakfast', it is simply broken up bread and butter with milk and sugar, and hot tea poured over.

siot: a thick oatcake, without fat, crushed fine in a bowl with cold buttermilk poured over.

troliod: dumplings made from oatmeal and fat skimmed from the top of broth, perhaps with a few currants. They were cooked in the broth and eaten instead of potatoes when they were scarce in Spring.

tocyn y Cardi: little 'cakes' made of flour and porridge oats with a little milk and a pinch of salt—fried with the bacon.

poten dato: boiled potatoes mixed with a little flour, sugar, spice, currants, butter, an egg and milk to give a soft consistency, baked in the oven when the bread had been removed. Children loved it, and it IS nice.

llymru: the liquor from oatmeal steeped in water for 24 hours, strained off, boiled and

Bibi Freeman 1982

thickened with flour, then left to go cold
and set. The English called it flummery
and enhanced it into a party dish with
sugar and flavourings.

cawl llaeth: skim milk, boiled and poured
on to a paste of oatmeal and cold water,
salted and boiled to thicken. Served in
bowls over barley bread.

tatws llaeth: potatoes (pref. new) boiled in
their skins, peeled and eaten from a bowl
with buttermilk poured over.

brŵes: breadcrumbs and oatmeal and a little butter or dripping seasoned with salt
and pepper with boiling water poured over.

limpet pie: boiled limpets, leeks and fatty
bacon cut in bits baked between bread
dough or shortcrust, sometimes with hard-
boiled eggs included.

sheep's head broth: the head a gift from
the farmer to his impoverished worker,
boiled with leeks and parsley and eaten
with oatmeal dumplings.

Ffagodau
FAGGOTS

	I	M	A
belly pork	2 lbs	1 kilo	2 lbs
pig's liver	1 lb	450g	1 lb
breadcrumbs	1½ lbs	¾ kilo	1½ lbs
onions or shallots	1½ lbs	¾ kilo	1½ lbs
good pinch sage, salt, pepper			
pig's caul (shawl)	stock		

Commercially-made faggots usually contain the lights, melt and heart to stretch the liver (which is now relatively expensive). In traditional domestic recipes the liver only is used, but in this one from N. Pembrokeshire, it is combined with belly pork to give an especially good result. Note: faggots are unknown in the US, where the word means a rather unsavoury tramp!

Mince the two meats and onions, mix with the crumbs and seasonings. Divide into 2in. balls and wrap each in a 5in. square of caul, or roll in flour. Place faggots in rows in a baking tin, pour over some good stock to come well up the faggots and bake 2 hours in a slow oven, adding more boiling water or stock if necessary to keep the faggots nearly covered.

Cacennau Caul Cymreig
WELSH CURD CAKES

	I	M	A
curd or cottage cheese	4 ozs	125g	½ cup
butter	2 ozs	50g	½ stick
sugar	1 oz	25g	1 tbls.
currants	1 oz	25g	⅛th cup
cake or biscuit crumbs	1 oz	25g	⅓rd cup

2 egg yolks   pinch salt   teas. brandy
grated rind of 1 lemon
6 ozs shortcrust pastry

Cream the butter and sugar, add yolks, currants, crumbs, curds and brandy. Fill, but do not over-fill, patty tins lined with pastry. Bake in a moderate oven (350°F; Gas 4; 180°C) about 15 minutes.

This is based on what I suspect is quite an old recipe which I found in *'Croeso Cymreig'*. Curds would be readily available when cheese was still made on the farms in Wales. Cottage cheese, or 1 pint of cut junket, will substitute successfully.

Teisen Hufen Patagonia
PATAGONIA CREAM TART

	I	M	A
flour	8 ozs	225g	1¼ cups
butter	4 ozs	125g	1 stick
double cream	½ pt	275 mls	1¼ cups
3 eggs			
1 tbls. vanilla sugar			

There are many such rich recipes from the Welsh colony in S. America, created by overplus of dairy produce. Rub the butter into the flour and bind with the egg yolks to a rich paste. Rest it for several hours before rolling out to line a fairly deep pie dish. Beat the egg whites until stiff, fold the cream with the sugar (use essence if vanilla sugar is not available), sprinkle nutmeg on top and bake in a slow oven (325°F, Gas 3, 170°C) for 35-40 mins.

Teisen Nionod
ONION CAKE

2 lb potatoes
1 or 2 onions
butter
pepper and salt
½ pt (275mls; 1¼ cups) beef stock (opt)

Another good country dish with a relative across the channel: *pommes de terre boulangère*. I don't quite know why in Wales it was made in a cake tin, but if you use waxy potatoes it may hold its shape like a cake when turned out. I use a heavy earthenware ovendish.

Grease the dish really well with butter. Thinly slice the potatoes (soak a few minutes in cold water to extract the starch), drain and dry before covering the bottom of the dish with a double layer of slices. Sprinkle finely-chopped onion on top, dot with butter, season with pepper and salt. Continue in this way until the dish is full, finishing with potatoes and extra butter. Pour in beef stock if liked, cover top with greaseproof paper and bake in a hot oven for about 1 hour. The potatoes should be soft right through and the top browned and crispy, so remove the paper after about ¾ hour.

Cawl Ffa
BROAD BEAN BROTH

	I	M	A
bacon (piece)	2 lb	1 kilo	2 lb
broad beans (shelled)	½ lb	225g	½ lb
potatoes	1 lb	450g	1 lb

swede turnip (small)
2 leeks
parsley   pinch sage

Soak the bacon overnight in cold water, then cover with fresh cold water, bring to the boil and skim. Add the potatoes and turnip, cut roughly, and when these are nearly done, the beans. Thicken with a paste of 1 tbls. oatmeal and water if liked, and sprinkle finely-chopped leeks and parsley on the top to serve.

Cacen Gneifio
SHEARING CAKE

	I	M	A
flour	8 ozs	225g	1¼ cups
moist brown sugar	6 ozs	175g	⅔rd cup
butter	4 ozs	125g	1 stick
milk	¼ pt.	150 mls	⅔ cup

1 teas. baking powder
2 teas. caraway seeds
rind of ½ lemon   grated nutmeg   1 egg

Sheep-shearing time, was, and still is, one of the major social occasions in Welsh rural life, for in the difficult hill country especially, farmers help each other on a rota basis with the rounding-up and shearing. The host farm kitchen is busy for days beforehand making pies and tarts and cakes and baked meats. Caraway seeds flavour this traditional cake. Sift the flour and baking powder, add the spice etc., rub in the butter, then work in the beaten egg and milk. Bake in a greased tin lined with paper in a mod. oven (350°F, Gas 4, 180°C) for 1 hour.

Note on Wine-making

Home wine-making techniques have changed so markedly in recent years that I have thought it better to adapt the old Welsh county wine recipes to modern methods. The main differences apply to the yeast and nutrient (the old way was yeast on a piece of toast floated on the must) and finers. Quantities of fruits and flowers etc and sugar remain much the same as in the original Welsh recipes. For more detailed information consult one of the many books on home winemaking, as space prevents giving too much detail here.

Gwin Rhiwbob
RHUBARB WINE

	I	M	A
rhubarb	3 lbs	1.25 kilos	2½ lbs
sugar	3 lbs	1.5 kilos	2½ lbs
raisins	1 lbs	450g	2½ cups
water	1 gall.	4.5 litre	1 gall.
yeast + nutrient			

Use young rhubarb (May) for preference. Chop the rhubarb, unpeeled. Cover the fruit with the sugar and leave 24 hours for the fruit to absorb the sugar. Strain off the resultant liquor, rinse out all remaining sugar, then make liquor up to 1 gallon with water. Add raisins, yeast and nutrient, cover and keep in a warm place for one week, then transfer liquor to a fermentation vessel, fit air lock and ferment out.

Diod Sinsir
GINGERBEER

Gingerbeer has always been popular in Wales, particularly as a non-alcoholic alternative to ordinary beer for men parched by the heat of the iron and steel works. There were two kinds: one was a gingered herb, or 'small' beer, the other was the more straightforward kind, made with root ginger.

Bruise 1 oz ginger, put it in one gallon of water, add 1½ lb (¾ kilo) sugar and boil for an hour. Skim. Pour over a sliced lemon and ¼ oz (1 teas.) cream of tartar. When cool, add 1 oz bakers' yeast (the dried variety will do) and leave, covered, for 2 days. Strain and bottle. Drink in 3 days.

Cwrw Cartref
HOME BREW

Home-brewed beer is a legend in rural Wales at least. Family recipes are jealously guarded. This one was given to me by my son-in-law's mother, who was famous for her home brew.

handful nettle tops
½ a bushel of malt
½ lb hops
5 gallons water
1 cup brewers' yeast or dried equivalent

Make a mash with the malt and a little boiling water. Leave overnight, covered. Boil the 5 galls. water, pour slowly over the malt mash in the cask with the bung-hole stopped with gorse in flower (if possible!) so the liquid seeps through this into a bowl. Boil for 1½ hours. Cool. Add hops and sugar, strain back into the (stopped) cask. Add the yeast when cool, leave 2-3 days. The top should clear after about 7 days: bottle and store.

Gwirod Blodyn Ysgaw
ELDERFLOWER CORDIAL

Friends have a curious habit of calling on me around elderflower time, not for the 'champagne', but for this cordial, which is simplicity itself to make. It just takes 24 hours, and you need some rose petals as well as about 20 heads of elderflowers, gathered in full sunlight. Boil 3 pints (1.8 litres; 7½ cups) water, and when cold, pour it over the flowers in a large bowl. Then add 2 ozs (50g; 2 teas.) tartaric acid and 2 lemons, thinly sliced. Sprinkle rose petals over the top. Stir every time you pass the bowl, and after 24 hours, strain and bottle. It will keep (given a chance!) quite a while, and is nicest diluted with soda-water. I use it to liquidise rose petals, too, to add to home-made Greek yoghurt and wild strawberries. . .

Fizz Blodyn Ysgaw
ELDERFLOWER FIZZ

Sometimes affectionately called elderflower 'champagne', this was popular 60 years ago in the country and is currently enjoying a revival due to the interest in country wine-making. It is very easy, but you do need some strong champagne-type bottles or cider flagons with heavy screw tops.

Boil 1 gallon (4 litres) of water and dissolve in it 1½ lbs (750g) sugar. When quite cold, add a few large heads of elderflower, gathered in full sun, and the rind and juice of a lemon, plus 2 tbls. wine vinegar. Cover with a thick cloth and leave 24 hours in a cool place. Squeeze the flowers, then strain through a fine sieve. Store as indicated—it will be ready to drink in about 2 weeks and will have satisfyingly intoxicating 'head'.

Gwin Danadl Poethion
NETTLE SYRUP

Do you, like me, grow nettles for the butterflies? Nettle tops (the 4 fresh new leaves only) are good to eat as a green vegetable, and they can be used to make this old-fashioned syrup for a base to be diluted with soda water to make a cooling drink.

Wash the nettle tops thoroughly. To every pound add two pints (5 cups) water. Boil for an hour, strain, and to every pint of juice add 1 lb sugar. Boil for 30 mins. Bottle when cold. From *'Croeso Cymreig'*.

NB wear rubber gloves when nettle-gathering!

Cacen Ddyrnu
THRESHING CAKE

	I	M	A
plain flour	1 lb	450g	3 cups
mixed currants & raisins	1 lb	450g	2¾ cups
sugar	8 ozs	225g	1 cup
bacon dripping or butter	8 ozs	225g	2 sticks
2-3 eggs 1 teas. bicarb. soda buttermilk to mix			

Threshing-time in the past in Wales had its traditional cake . . . note the use of buttermilk and bacon fat, often used in cake-making in Wales, for there was always plenty of both.

Dissolve the bicarb. soda in a little tepid water mixed with some of the buttermilk. Add the beaten eggs with the soda mixture and enough buttermilk to give a fairly soft consistency. Bake in a greased cake tin in a fairly hot oven (400°F, Gas 6, 200°C) for about 1½ hours.

AUTUMN

Leeks in Summer

The inclusion of leeks in what were obviously
summer-time Welsh recipes defeated me at first.
Not being country born and bred I did not
realise that substitutes for the winter variety
were to be had in country gardens—hollow
leeks, chives, perpetual leeks, spring onions,
shallots, and holly leeks (not to be confused with
'hollow' leeks) are all loosely referred to in
Wales as 'leeks'. Also, the tops of new (annual)
leeks would be cut off as they pushed through
the ground; this it was claimed, would
encourage the leeks to grow stouter.

But beware of using perpetual leeks when they
are old, as they are then extremely 'woody' and
unpleasant.

Swper Mam
MUM'S SUPPER

8 bacon or ham rashers
2 onions, finely chopped
4 ozs (125g, 1¼ cups) grated cheese
pepper and salt

Variations on the bacon theme are endless in
Welsh cookery. No wonder, with a pig in every
backyard! This quickly-made dish is comforting
on a cold winter's night—hence its name?

Layer bacon, onion and cheese in a shallow,
oven-proof dish, seasoning each layer and ending
with a layer of bacon. Bake in a hot oven 30
mins. or until the top bacon is crisp. Good with
jacket potatoes.

Gŵydd Mihangel
MICHAELMAS GOOSE

A feast of the old days, from the farmer to his tenants when they paid their rents, its style of cooking born of the one pot over the fire tradition. After the harvest the geese were turned on to the fields to glean: they fattened quickly. Goosefeather beds helped keep out the cold in Welsh hill-farm bedrooms; some of the bigger feathers were used in the kitchen—the large wing pinion for sweeping the hearth, the smaller wing feathers for brushing flour or oatmeal while baking.

For this *cawl* the prepared goose was simply boiled in plenty of water with a bowlful of chopped onions, salt and pepper, and thickened with oatmeal. The thick, fatty broth was just what was wanted then to keep out the cold. . .but not today, perhaps. As an alternative, try giving a goose the *bain marie* treatment, as with the salt duck, saving the lovely white fat for baking or frying—or for rubbing into a tight chest as in former days.

Pwdin Pysennau
PEAS PUDDING

1½ pints split peas
2 ozs butter
2 eggs
pepper and salt

This traditional old British dish is popular today in Wales in its present form made from dried peas and often called 'mushy peas'. But the original was more substantial, and made from split peas. Soak the peas overnight in water. Next day, tie them loosely in a clean cloth, leaving room for them to well. Put them to boil in cold water for about 2½ hours. When tender, press through a sieve with a wooden spoon, then add the other ingredients and beat all together. Tie again in a floured cloth and boil for another hour. Serve very hot.

Tarten Bwmpen
MARROW PIE

one marrow
cupful sugar
cupful currants
sprinkle vinegar
pinch ginger
a few cloves
shortcrust pastry

Most Welsh recipe collections include one for marrow in a pie, spiced and often mixed with a little apple. No water is needed as the marrow supplies a lot of moisture.

Peel and slice the marrow, discarding seeds. Line a deep pie dish with shortcrust, fill with marrow, interlayered with sugar, currants and spices and a sprinkle of (wine) vinegar. Cover with a pastry lid. Bake in a moderate oven until the marrow is cooked (325°F, Gas 3, 170°C). Or you can cook the marrow first, drain, then bake the pie in a hotter oven, more quickly.

Poten Ben Fedi
POTATO HARVEST PUDDING

2 lbs potatoes
1 cup (breakfast) minced cooked meat
1 large bacon rasher
1 onion
knob butter
1 tbls. wholewheat flour

Boil and mash the potatoes with the butter and flour. Cut up the rasher of bacon, fry it with the finely chopped onion, then add both, with the minced meat, to the mashed potatoes. Season with salt and pepper, mix thoroughly and turn into a greased pie dish and bake in a moderate oven for about 20 minutes until the top is nice and golden.

This was a traditional Sunday supper dish for the time in late September/October when the potato harvest had been brought in.

Katt Pies

	I	M	A
flour	1 lb	450g	1 lb
suet or lard	6 ozs	175g	2 cups*
milk & water	¼ pt	150mls	⅔ cup
minced mutton or lamb	½ lb	225g	½ lb
currants	½ lb	225g	1 cup
brown sugar	½ lb	225g	1 cup
salt and pepper			

Mutton pies like these were great favourites with the British; spiced and sweetened with sugar and dried fruit, the taste of tainted meat was disguised. Katt pies were associated with Templeton (Pembrokeshire) Fair, but the name is a great puzzle as there is no letter 'k' in the Welsh alphabet. Make a hot water crust with the fat, milk and water and flour and use this to make individual pies about 4in. diameter. Arrange the filling in layers, seasoning as you go, then close the pie with a pastry lid. Bake 30 mins. in a hot oven (425°F, Gas 7, 220°C). Best eaten hot.

* applies to suet only

Pastai Gwningen
RABBIT PIE

	I	M	A
1 rabbit			
beefsteak	½ lb	225g	½ lb
cooked ham	¼ lb	125g	¼ lb
shortcrust or puff pastry			
stock			
2 teas. chopped parsley			
nutmeg, pepper and salt			

The seasoning of nutmeg gives a clue to the age of this nice old pie, the recipe coming perhaps from a *plas* or a well-to-do farm. Soak the rabbit in cold, salted water for a few hours. Joint, and place in a pie dish with the ham and steak cut in small pieces. Sprinkle with the parsley and seasonings, add enough stock just to cover and put a pastry lid on top. Bake in a very moderate oven 1½ hours, covering the pastry with paper or foil if it becomes too brown.

Teisennau Llanddarog
LLANDDAROG FAIR CAKES

	I	M	A
SR flour	12 ozs	350g	2½ cups
butter	8 ozs	225g	2 sticks
sugar	6 ozs	175g	¾ cup
beer ¾ tbls.			
currants			

Llanddarog was on one of the old drovers' routes, and the cakes, made with beer which helped them to keep well, were popular with the drovers for their long journeys to the English grazing lands and markets. They were about 6in. long, 3in. wide, ¼in. thick, marked like dominoes with the currants, and cost 2d each.

Mix flour and sugar together and rub in the butter. Make to a stiff dough with beer, roll out to ¼in. thick and cut into rectangles. Bake in a mod. oven for 20-30 mins. until golden. Makes about 24.

Bara Mwyar
BLACKBERRY BREAD PUDDING

blackberries
sugar
stale bread

So simple, yet so deliciously different, this is one of my favourites. It has charmed and intrigued the most sophisticated gourmets. Quantities are immaterial.

Set blackberries to stew over a low heat and when the juice is flowing nicely, add sugar to taste. Now throw in pieces of torn bread (a mixture of half brown and half white is much the best) until the juice is all but absorbed—not too much bread or the result will be stodgy. Chill very thoroughly and serve with plenty of double cream.

This pudding can be made just as successfully with tinned or frozen blackberries.

Jeli Criafol
ROWANBERRY JELLY

The proportions for this glorious, glowing-red accompaniment for roast lamb or roast pork are: 1 lb (450g) sugar to 1 pint (575mls; 2½ cups) juice, with the juice of a lemon to each pint of liquid. 3 lbs berries stewed with 1½ pints water will yield about a pint of juice. Some make it with apples, or crabapples, but this produces a pinky, clouded jelly, not as attractive in my view. A pinch of ginger adds interest to the flavour.

Gather rowanberries when they have turned to deep red, indicating they are fully ripe. Strip the berries from the main stalks—do not worry about the smaller ones as they will be caught in the straining. Simmer berries until tender, strain overnight in a jelly-bag. Then make as for a jelly in the above proportions.

Brithyllod Rhost
BAKED TROUT WITH OATMEAL

1 trout per person
fine or medium oatmeal
bacon dripping
salt and pepper

Clean and gut the trout, with or without heads and tails. Melt bacon dripping in an overproof dish. Season the oatmeal with salt and fresh-ground pepper. Dry the trout, then roll in the oatmeal. Fit the fish side by side in the dish, dot with bacon fat. Cover with foil or lid, bake about 30 mins. in a moderate oven. Remove covering to brown for 10 mins. more. (250°F, Gas 4, 180°C)

Swper Sgadan
SUPPER HERRINGS

4 medium herring
1 large apple
6 med. potatoes
1 large onion
1 heaped teas. made mustard
1 teas. chopped fresh sage
good knob butter
3 tbls. tarragon vinegar
hot water or cider
salt   freshly-ground black pepper

Clean and fillet the fish. Spread insides with mustard, season and roll up. Line a greased fireproof dish with sliced potatoes, sliced onions, and thirdly, sliced apples. Sit the rolled fillets on top, sprinkle with sage, vinegar and seasoning. Cover with the remaining potatoes. Half fill the dish with cider or water. Dot with butter, cover and bake in a mod. oven for 45 mins. Remove lid to let the top brown for a further 30 mins.

Bara Lawr
LAVERBREAD

Visitors to SW Wales, if they are lucky, may be offered little 'cakes' of laverbread with their breakfast bacon and eggs. Enjoyment of this edible seaweed, found on west coasts, is truly traditional in Wales, many people still gathering it and boiling it themselves as part of their household routine. But it is more often bought in the markets, ready prepared. 'Laverbread' is a misnomer, and sets many people seeking a loaf, but it is just a literal translation of the Welsh—with the *'bara'* in this context meaning sustenance rather than bread. To make the little cakes or patties for breakfast, prepared laver is mixed with medium oatmeal to help hold the shape and then fried in bacon fat. It can also be dressed with a little olive oil and lemon juice and eaten with dry toast, or added to a white sauce, or mixed with orange juice and meat gravy, as a sauce.

Cawl Lawr
LAVER SOUP

This is in no way traditional, but a suggestion of cookery writer Jane Grigson. It is very good indeed. Make a good vegetable soup with a chicken or mutton stock. Stir in 2 tbls. prepared laver per pint, simmer 5 mins., then liquidise. The result is a soup of an interesting green colour which looks even better with a swirl of cream and the addition of *croûtons*.

54

Gwin Ysgaw
ELDERBERRY WINE

	I	M	A
elderberries	7 lbs	3 kilos (approx)	7 lbs
sugar	3 lbs	1.5 kilos	3 lbs
seedless raisins	1 lb	450g	2¾ cups
ground ginger	½ oz	15g	1 teas.
citric acid	1 teas.	1 teas.	1 teas.
6 cloves			
water	3 gal.	13.5 l.	3 gal.
yeast + nutrient			

Put the berries, stripped from their stalks with the prongs of a fork, in a large bowl and pour over 3 gallons boiling water. Leave 24 hours. Mash the fruit, strain through a jelly bag. Add the sugar, ginger, raisins and cloves to the juice and boil gently for 1 hour. Cool, add yeast. Leave to ferment in a dark place or in dark bottles for about 2 weeks until fermentation subsides a little. Then put in jars with airlocks and ferment out. Leave at least 3 months, preferably 12, before drinking. This Welsh recipe gives a rounder result than usual.

Gwin Panasan
PARSNIP WINE

This wine can be difficult to clear if care is not taken to keep the parsnips from becoming mushy or pressing them to hasten straining.

	I	M	A
parsnips	7 lbs	3 kilos	5½ lbs
water	2½ galls	11 litres	2½ galls
juice of 1 lemon and 1 orange			
yeast + nutrient.			
pectic enzyme			

Scrape parsnips, slice and boil in half the water until tender but not mushy. Strain, measure liquor, add 3 lbs sugar to the gallon. Bring to the boil, simmer ¾ hour, add citric juices. Turn into a bucket, cool to 21°C, add yeast + nutrient and pectic enzyme. Cover with a thick cloth, leave in a warm place 2 weeks, stirring from the bottom daily. Strain into fermenting jars, fit air locks, leave 6 months in a cooler place to clear. Syphon off, bottle, keep 6 months.

Gwin Mwyar Duon
BLACKBERRY WINE

Pick the blackberries when fully ripe on a dry day. Make sure they are maggot-free. Wash and crush in a plastic bucket.

	I	M	A
blackberries	4 lbs	1.75 kilos	3 lbs
sugar	3 lbs	1.5 kilos	2¼ lbs
water	1 gall	4.5 litres	1 gall
yeast + nutrient			
pectic enzyme			

Pour boiling water over the crushed fruit, cool to 21°C, then add pectic enzyme, next day the yeast and nutrient, maintaining temperature. Cover closely, leave 4-5 days, stirring daily. Strain through a sieve on to the sugar, making sure it is thoroughly dissolved. This wine will produce a lively fermentation so do not fill the fementation jar above its shoulder, reserving the spare liquor in a bottle with a plug of cotton wool. When the foaming dies down, add this to the main jar. Leave until the wine clears, then rack—several rackings may be required for a really clear wine.

Gwin Afalau
APPLE WINE

	I	M	A
apples	6 lbs	2.75 kilos	5 lbs
sugar	2.2 lbs	1 kilo	2¼ lbs
lemons	2	2	2
water	1 gall.	4.5 litre	1 gall.

piece of bruised ginger
a few colves
yeast + nutrient

Windfall apples will do. Wash and cut up, skins, cores and all—even brown patches. Put over boiling water, crush fruit, simmer 10-15 mins. Strain on to sugar and thinly peeled lemon rind. Add lemon juice, cloves and bruised ginger. Cool to 21°C, add yeast and nutrient, cover and leave 24 hours in a warm place. Put into a fermenting jar, insert air lock, leave 4 weeeks. Syphon off and mature for a further 6 weeks before bottling.

Pwdin Efa
EVE'S PUDDING

	I	M	A
stewed apples, sweetened			
plain flour	2 ozs	50g	½ cup
sugar	1 oz	25g	⅛ cup
butter	1½ ozs	38g	⅓ stick
milk	½-¾ pt.	275-425 mls	1½-2 cups

2 eggs, separated

The soufflé topping to this apple-based pudding demands immediate eating from the oven, for it collapses very quickly. Grease a deep, straight-sided oven-proof dish, cover the bottom with a generous layer of cooked apple. Melt the butter, in a saucepan, stir in the flour, add the milk gradually to make a smooth sauce. Pour into a bowl and add the sugar and egg yolks. Fold in the stiffly-beaten egg whites. Pour over the apples, bake for ¾ hour in a fairly hot oven (425°F, Gas 7, 220°C).

Sinsir Afal
APPLE GINGER

	I	M	A
apples	4 lbs	1¾ K	4 lbs
gran. sugar	2 lbs	1 K	4½ cups
lump sugar	4 lbs	1¾ K	4 lbs
root ginger	2 ozs	50g	4 inches
3 lemons			
½ teas. cayenne pepper			
water	1 pint	20 fl.ozs	2½ cups

Peel, core and quarter the apples. Make a syrup from 2 lbs granulated sugar in 1 pt. of water. Let it boil, then pour over the apples. Let it stand for two days. Add 4 lbs lump sugar, the rind and juice of the lemons. Bruise the ginger in a bag, then add, together with the cayenne, bring to the boil, simmer about an hour until the juice is quite clear. Strain and pot when jelling point is reached.

This old-fashioned preserve is probably early 18th century.

Bara Gwenith
WHOLEWHEAT BREAD

	I	M	A
wholewheat flour	2 lbs	900g	2 lbs
1 tbls. oil or butter	1 oz	25g	¼ stick
2 teas. dried yeast + scant teas. sugar			
2 teas. salt			
warm water	1 pint	575mls	2½ cups

For a lighter, less dense loaf, use ⅓ white flour to ⅔rds brown. The literal translation of *gwenith* is 'wheat', but the most usual everyday bread in Wales was what we now carefully call 'wholewheat'. The Real Bread movement is very vigorous in Wales today.

Froth the yeast with the sugar and a little warm water. Add the salt to the warmed flour, make a well in the centre, add the oil or butter (melted), then the yeast and enough warmed water to make a workable dough. Knead. Give this one or two rises according to preference (more rises, better texture). Bake in a hot oven, lowering the heat after 20 minutes, and again 20 mins later.

Teisen Sinsir
GINGER CAKE

	I	M	A
butter	4 ozs	125g	1 stick
brown sugar	2 ozs	50g	¼ cup
black treacle	1 lb	450g	1 lb
flour	1 lb	450g	5⅛ cups
milk	¼ pt	150mls	⅔ cup
candied peel	1 oz	25g	1 tbls.
ground ginger	1 oz	25g	1 tbls.
bicarb. soda 1 teas.	2 eggs		

Warm the treacle, butter and sugar together. Cut the peel finely and add to the dry ingredients. Beat the eggs, add to the treacle mixture, combine with the flour etc with milk to make a loose mixture. Pour into a shallow, well-greased tin, bake ¾ hour in a mod. oven (350°F, Gas 4, 180°C).

The daily chore of fetching the water, Carno (Montgomeryshire)

Medd
MEAD

Unless you have access to a plentiful supply of honey, this ancient brew is nowdays prohibitively expensive to make, a situation for which the increased use of insecticides is to blame. Using the honey-comb after the honey has been extracted is a cheaper alternative which was in fact a commonplace amongst ordinary folk—it also results in a mead of less cloying sweetness. This method is from Mattie Thomas' MS on traditional Welsh food (held in the NLW at Aberystwyth). She says it was brewed in June and kept in large earthenware jars buried in boggy land until the following Spring.

Put the empty comb in a large bowl, pour a gallon of cold water over and allow to steep overnight. Next day, filter through a wine sieve into a cooker. Boil over a slow fire, skimming regularly. When it boils, add a handful of hops and boil ¼ hour. Cool to 20°C, add 1 pint brewers' yeast or yeast + nutrient. Cover with a cloth and ferment overnight. Next day, skim the surface, transfer to jars and cork.

Gwin Persli
PARSLEY WINE

	I	M	A
parsley (no stalks)	1 lb	450 g	1 lb
demerera sugar	4 lbs	1.75 kilos	3 lbs
water	1 gall	4.5 litres	1 gall
2 oranges, 2 lemons			
yeast + nutrient			

Boil the parsley in a muslin bag with the thinly peeled orange and lemon rind. Simmer ½ hour. Squeeze bag and take from pan. Add sugar and fruit juices. Cool to 21°C, add yeast and nutrient, put in fermentation jar, fit airlock and ferment out.

WINTER

Crempog Furum
YEAST PANCAKES

	I	M	A
plain flour or oatmeal	12 ozs	350g	3 cups

1 teas. dried yeast
3 tbls. sugar
2 eggs
milk or buttermilk
salt   large knob butter

These are well worth making, especially with oatmeal, for a change. Mix the yeast with a little of the sugar and some warm water and leave to sponge. Heat the milk or buttermilk and dissolve the butter in it. Mix the flour, sugar and salt, make a well in the centre and pour the beaten eggs in. Gradually add the milk, beating well to make a soft, creamy batter. Lastly add the yeast mixture—leave to rise in a warm place. Make as pancakes in the usual way, splitting in half when finished and spreading with butter. Serve warm.

Pancosen Fawr
LARGE PANCAKE

Welsh cookery is full of recipes for pancakes and batter puddings—one like this was used on the toad-in-the-hole principle, i.e. a 'filler' or 'stretcher' for the meat.

	I	M	A
SR flour	6 ozs	175 g	1 cup+
sugar	2 ozs	50 g	2 tbls

1 egg
pinch bicarbonate of soda
milk to mix

Mix the dry ingredients together. Beat the egg and add to the flour etc with the milk in the usual way to make a fairly thick batter.

In a heavy frying pan cook four silces of home-cured Welsh ham (this may be obtainable in country markets), keep hot when done. Pour the batter into the hot fat and cook carefully on both sides until golden brown. Cut into four, place a silce of ham on each and serve immediately.

Teisen Fala
APPLE CAKE

	I	M	A
SR flour	10 ozs	275g	2 cups
butter	5 ozs	150g	1¼ sticks
brown sugar	5 ozs	150g	¾ cup
cooking apples	1 lb	450g	1 lb
milk to mix			

This is unexpectedly delicious, especially when eaten warm with lots of cream. The mixture can also be divided into a bun tray to make what the English call 'apple muffins'.

Rub the fat into the flour, add the sugar. Peel and core the apples and cut into tiny dice. Mix all together with a little milk to bind to a fairly stiff dough. Spread into a well-greased shallow tin and bake for about 30 mins. in a moderate oven (350°F, Gas 4, 180°C).

Tatws Popty
BAKED POTATOES

An old favourite in Wales, perhaps more associated with N Wales than in other parts, and mentioned as the variation when the par-boiled potatoes are cooked under the reasting joint in *'Adam's Luxury & Eve's Cookery'* (1744). In this version the potatoes are cooked in the roasting tin after the joint has been taken out. Pour away all excess fat, then fill the tin with potatoes, thickly sliced lengthways, then cover with a layer of finely-chopped onion. Season with pepper and salt, sprinkle a little flour over and cover with boiling water. Roast in a hot oven until the potatoes are golden brown.

Bara Pyglyd
PIKELETS

	I	M	A
plain strong white flour	1 lb	450g	2½ cups
½ milk ½ water, mixed	1 pt	575mls	2½ cups
1 teas. dried yeast			
1 dstp. sea salt			
1 teas. sugar 2 tbls. oil			

The English name is probably a corruption of the Welsh. 'Pitchy bread' was another name for them. They resemble the thicker English crumpet in their mixture but are not cooked in rings. The Welsh love holey breads for they hold so much lovely golden butter.

Warm the flour, add salt. Warm the oil, milk/water, sugar to blood heat (use a little to cream the yeast), add to the flour to make a yeasty batter, beating well until quite smooth. Cover bowl, leave to rise at room temperature 1½-2 hours until well up the bowl and covered with bubbles. Beat down with a spoon, cover again in a warm place to recover (30 mins.). Cook pikelets one at a time (about 6in. across) on a lightly-greased, moderately hot griddle. The holes appear very quickly. Cook both sides to a pale brown colour.

Bara Cymysg
MASLIN BREAD

	I	M	A
wheatmeal flour	20 ozs	575g	4 cups
rye flour	4 ozs	125g	scant cup
warm water (approx)	½ pint	425mls	1¼ cups
1 tbls. veg. oil			
2 teas. salt			
1 teas. dried yeast + 1 teas. sugar dissolved in a little warm water			

Maslin was the old name for bread made from mixed grains, deriving from early times when a mix of grains were sown as an insurance against total crop failure. Success meant a mixed crop and bread for the lower orders. However, the mix I've developed here is addictively delicious—close-textured and slightly malty.

Make in the usual way, giving the dough (a very pleasant, pliable one) two risings. Bake 15 mins. in a hot oven, then reduce to mod. for a further 20-30 mins. Makes one 3lb loaf or one 2 lb & one 1lb, or three 1lb.

Pwdin Reis Mamgu
GRANDMOTHER'S RICE PUDDING

	I	M	A
rice	2 ozs	50g	⅓ cup
demerara sugar	2 ozs	50g	¼ cup
Jersey milk or single cream	1 pt.	575 mls	2½ cups
butter	1 oz	25g	¼ stick
water	½ pt.	275 mls	1¼ cups
2 eggs + 2 whites			
4 tbls. caster sugar			
nutmeg pinch salt			

An old, and much grander version of its unfortunate poor relation, nursery rice pudding. Simmer the rice in the water until the grains are swollen. Add milk or cream, butter, sugar and salt and nutmeg, and the beaten yolks of eggs. Whisk the 4 egg whites until stiff, folding in the caster sugar—pile this meringue on top of the pudding and bake in a moderate oven for ½ hour (350°F, Gas 4, 180°C) until the meringue is pale, biscuity colour.

Pwdin Moronen Patagonia
PATAGONIA CARROT PUDDING

	I	M	A
grated carrot			
grated potato			
raisins	8 ozs	225g	1¼ cups
plain flour			
sugar			
melted butter	4 ozs	125g	½ cup
½ teas. bicarb. of soda pinch salt			
2 teas. cinnamon			

When carrots are used in puddings and cakes it is for their sweetness, and the recipe an old one from the time when sugar was scarce and dear. The older the carrots the more sweetness they contain.

Mix the bicarb. with the potato. Add the raisins to the flour, then add all the other ingredients and mix together thoroughly. Turn into a greased basin, cover the top with foil or greaseproof paper and boil for 2 hours.

Eidion Sbeis
SPICED BEEF

10 lbs salt beef
1 dstp. black pepper
½ teas. ginger
1 saltspoon ground cloves
1 saltspoon nutmeg
½ saltspoon ground mace
1 glass claret or port

A recipe very similar to this, which is Mrs Beeton's, appears in some old Welsh recipe collections—with the wine or port ommitted. It is not of course particular to Wales, but would have been prepared in better-off Welsh households as elsewhere. The spices are mixed together before sprinkling over the meat, which is then rolled and skewered into shape before fitting into a casserole and the wine poured over. A tight-fitting lid must be used as no steam must escape during the 4-hour cooking in a slow oven. The meat is finally placed between two boards or plates with a weight on top. When cold, slice thinly to serve.

Pastai Gwydd
GOOSE PIE

There are rumours of an elaborate goose pie being made, on the Yorkshire pattern, in the mid 1800's (when they were fashionable for the Christmas trade) in Llansanffraid ym Mechain, Montgomery, near the Shropshire border. To make it today, do as Jane Grigson suggests in her adaptation in 'English Food' and use a hot water crust rather than the excessively thick crust designed to withstand the journey to London.

"Raise your crust just big enough to hold a large goose; first have a pickled dried tongue boiled tender to peel, cut off the root, bone a goose and a large fowl; take half a quarter of an ounce of mace beat fine, a large teaspoonful of beaten pepper, three teaspoonfulls of salt; mix together, season your fowl, and the goose in the same form as if whole. Put half a pound of butter on the top, and lay on the lid. This pie is delicious, either hot or cold, and will keep a great while. A slice of this pye cut down across makes a pretty little side-dish for supper."

Cacen Gri
SPECKLED CAKE

	I	M	A
flour	1 lb	450g	5⅓ cups
butter	6 oz	175g	1½ sticks

1 teas. each baking powder and bicarb. soda
1 egg
few currants
sugar to taste   milk to mix

This stiffish mixture is usually made as one cake on the bakestone (griddle), but it is also recorded as made in a pile, like a pile of pancakes, with plenty of good, salty Welsh butter plastered on each round. Mix the raising agents with the flour and rub in the butter. Add currants and sugar. Beat the egg into the milk and make the whole into a dough which can be rolled out fairly thinly. Cut into rounds about 4 in. across.

Teisennau Reis Gradell
RICE GRIDDLE CAKES

boiled rice	1 teacupful
flour	1 teacupful
milk	1 teacupful
butter	1 tbls.
salt	1 teas.
baking powder	1 teas.
1 egg	

Sieve the baking powder and flour together. Melt the butter and mix all together, stirring well. Drop large tablespoonfuls on to a hot, well-greased bakestone, griddle (or heavy frying pan) and cook about 4 mins. each side. Serve very hot with golden syrup.

Caws Pobi
ROASTED CHEESE

This is the true 'Welsh Rarebit' as far as the Welsh are concerned. They were inordinately fond of it from the earliest times in its simple form: later it developed into one of the many regional 'rarebits' or 'rabbits' as a cheese sauce on toast.

The original was simply a piece of hard cheese roasted, or toasted, on one side only, before the fire, on a piece of barley or other wholegrain bread. Now with the microwave we can take a gigantic backward leap across the centuries, for nothing makes *caws pobi* more correctly and faster than a few seconds in the MW.

Stwns Rwdan a Iau
MASHED TURNIPS & LIVER

	I	M	A
liver	1 lb	450g	1 lb
stock	½ pt.	275 mls	1¼ cups
2 medium onions			
flour fat for frying			
swede turnips			
old potatoes			

A *stwns* or mash of turnips and potatoes, well peppered and salted and with a good knob of butter worked in, is a welcome dish on a winter's day. In N Wales it was frequently combined with a dish of liver and onions: roll slices of liver in seasoned flour, then brown in hot fat. Remove to a casserole. Chop onion finely, fry till golden brown. Add to liver. Shake a little flour into the pan with more fat if needed, and brown, scraping up all the nice brown tasty bits before adding stock to make a good gravy. Add to the liver and cook covered in a mod. oven until the liver is tender, about 45 mins.

GROCER AND TEA DEALER.

Cawl Wystrys Gŵyr
GOWER OYSTER SOUP

	I	M	A
oysters	6 doz	70	70
mutton broth	4 pts	80 fl ozs	10 cups
butter	2 ozs	50g	½ stick
flour	1½ ozs	30g	¼ cup
cream	½ pt	275 mls	1¼ cups
salt cayenne mace			

Not traditional, in fact attributable to Mrs Beeton, but associated with Gower and its Victorian hotel trade and the one-time thriving oyster industry at Oystermouth.

Season the stock and bring to the boil. Meanwhile, work the butter and flour together to a paste (*beurre manié*), to add to the boiling stock in small pieces, stirring briskly to thicken. Simmer 5 mins. Pour over the oysters, re-heat but do not boil. Stir in heated cream—or milk if the soup is preferred less rich.

Gwydd y Calan
NEW YEAR'S GOOSE

In the earlier yeats of the last century, New Year's Day was much more of a festive occasion then Christmas Day, which was primarily a religious occasion. The traditional New Year dinner featured a boiled goose accompanied by a baked potato pudding and followed by rice pudding.

The goose was simmered over the fire with lots of chopped onions and parlsey for about 3 hours. Not perhaps to our taste today, unless the goose is separated from the greasy liquor, which is discarded.

Pwdin Cymreig
WELSH PUDDING

	I	M	A
butter	8 ozs	225g	2 sticks
sugar	6 ozs	175g	scant cup
8 small egg yolks			
4 small egg whites			
peel of a lemon			
puff paste			

At one time all baked puddings were encased in puff paste—our baked custard tarts of today are a reminder. This old recipe has some similarity with the original Bakewell pudding—you could put some jam or lemon curd over the pastry to enhance it. Melt the butter, beat the egg yolks into it, then the sugar; lastly fold in the stiffly-beaten egg whites. Add grated lemon peel. Line an ovenproof dish with puff pastry, pour the mixture in and bake it in a moderate oven for about an hour.

WASSAIL BOWL FOR ST DAVID'S DAY

The immense silver bowl in which this is traditionally served was given by Sir Watkin Williams Wynne, of the distinguished family which established itself at Plas Peniarth, Tywyn, Meirionnydd, to Jesus College, Oxford in 1732 in celebration of St David, Wales' patron saint.

It is basically a spiced beer: put ½ lb sugar into a bowl, pour over a pint of warm beer. Grate a little nutmeg and ginger over the mixture, then add 4 glasses of sherry and another 5 pints of beer. Stir, check for sweetness, adding more sugar if necessary, then leave, covered, for 2-3 hours. To serve: float roasted apples on the creaming mixture in the bowl.

Teisen Lap
MOIST CAKE

	I	M	A
sour cream	1 pt	575ml	2½ cups
butter	3 ozs	75g	¾ stick
sugar	4 ozs	125g	4 tbls.
sultanas	4 ozs	125g	gen. ½ cup
SR flour	3 ozs	75g	¾ cup
1 egg			

The earliest version was a 'batter cake', made with sour cream and baked in a Dutch oven before the fire until it was nice and scrunchy—often to use up cream which was insufficient for a churning of butter. The later, basic fruit cake was usually baked on an enamel plate, as *teisen blât* (plate cake). Because of its moistness it was popular with miners for their 'snaptin'.

Rub the butter into the flour, add the sugar and sultanas, beat the egg into the cream and mix thoroughly. Pour into a shallow tin and bake in a low oven (250° F, Gas ½, 130° C) or in a low position under a fairly hot grill.

Pwdin Ferw Sinsir
BOILED GINGER PUDDING

	I	M	A
SR flour	6 ozs	175g	scant cup
butter	2 ozs	50g	½ stick
sugar	2 ozs	50g	2 tbls.
milk	½ pint	275ml	1¼ cups
1 teas. ground ginger			

Old-fashioned boiled puddings are finding favour again as nostalgia for the past increases. Early boiled puddings were made with breadcrumbs, then flour, and boiled in a floured cloth. With the use of the basin, the cloth became the top covering. This is the plainest of recipes.

Warm the milk and butter together, then pour into the dry ingredients. Mix well before pouring into a well-greased basin. Cover and boil about 1½ hours in a saucepan half filled with water. Top up with boiling water as necessary.

Pwdin Eryri
SNOWDON PUDDING

	I	M	A
suet	½ lb	225g	1¼ cups
breadcrumbs	1 lb	450g	5¼ cups
lemon marmalade	6 oz	175g	6 ozs
pale brown sugar	6 ozs	175g	6 tbls.
rice flour	1½ ozs	35g	1½ tbls.

6 eggs 2 lemons some fine stoned raisins

Eliza Acton gave the 'genuine' recipe in 1845 (*Modern Cookery for Private Families*) asserting it to be 'constantly served to travellers at the hotel at the foot of Snowdon'—the 'Pen-y-groes'.

Butter a quart mould or basin thickly. Ornament it with the raisins pressed well into the butter. Mix the dry ingredients, blend with the well-beaten eggs. Put in the basin, boil 1½ hours. Half this quantity will fill a pint basin and take 1 hour to boil. Serve with a wine sauce.

Pwdin Watcyn Wynne
SIR WATKIN WILLIAMS WYNNE'S PUDDING

	I	M	A
suet	4 ozs	125g	¾ cup
sugar	4 ozs	125g	½ cup
breadcrumbs	4 ozs	125g	1½ cups

1 lemon   2 eggs, separated

A famous old bread pudding from the family whose name is much in evidence along the Cheshire/Shropshire border with Wales.

Grate the lemon rind, strain the juice. Add the beaten egg yolks to all the other ingredients, then fold in the stiffly-beaten egg whites. Steam 2 hours in a mould or buttered basin. Serve with a sauce of 2 egg yolks, 1 tbls. sugar, 1 tbls. brandy, rum or whiskey, 2 tbls. warm water, whisked over a low heat until stiff. Use immediately.

Pwdin Lemwn Owain Glyndŵr
OWEN GLENDOWER'S LEMON PUDDING

'so named (and Anglicised) by Sir Robert Howel Vaughan, Bart, the real
composer Certain'.

3 lemons (juice & zest)
3 tbls. chopped suet
14 tbls. white breadcrumbs
6 tbls caster sugar
3 tbls. white wine or cider
1 egg yolk
currants

This is a modern adaptation of a late 18th century recipe from a MS
cookery book compiled at the Vaughan mansion near Dolgellau, where
the heroic Welsh freedom fighter held one of his two parliaments.
Mix all the ingredients together, adding the eggs last, and either fill
small, well-greased oven-proof dishes, or one large dish, and bake,
covered, in a water-bath in a moderate oven (350°F; Gas 4; 180°C)
¾ hr. or longer for the single dish.
(Sauce for the puddings: butter, white wine, sugar and lemon juice
boiled together for a few minutes.)

Cacen Ddu Patagonia
PATAGONIA BLACK CAKE

	I	M	A
butter	10 ozs	275g	2½sticks
dark brown sugar	10 ozs	275g	1½ cups
raisins, sultanas, currants, of each	8 ozs	225g	1½ cups
mixed peel	6 ozs	175g	gen. cup
chopped nuts (walnuts or almonds)	4 ozs	125g	1½ cups
plain flour	1 lb	450g	1 lb

4 eggs
1 teas. each cinnamon and mixed spice
2 teas. baking powder
1 teas. almond essence / small glass rum
1 teas. bicarb. soda mixed into
1 teas. vinegar + 1 tbls. water

One might take this to be just another rich, dark fruit cake, until it comes to the final stage of enbalming it in a crisp casing of thin icing. It then becomes reminiscent of the Black Bun of Scotland. What makes it unmistakably South American is the rum. This is a cake which can be made well ahead of times of celebration, and kept, in cool conditions, maturing for months.

Grease and line an 8in cake tin. Cream the butter and sugar, adding the lightly whisked eggs a little at a time, beating well. Fold in the sieved flour and spices, the dried fruit and nuts. Pour the liquid with the 2 raising agents, together with the almond essence, on to the mixture and mix thoroughly. Lastly add the rum.

Bake on the middle shelf of a moderate oven (325°F, Gas 3, 170°C) for 3-3½ hours.

For the casing:
6 ozs icing sugar (175g, scant cup) mixed with 3 tbls. hot water as a thin, glacé-type icing. Brush all over the cake—top, sides and bottom—to completely encase it in a brittle sugar shell. This is easier to do while the cake is still warm.

Hwyad Hallt Cymreig
WELSH SALT DUCK

a full-size duck (6 lb in weight if possible)
onions   bay leaf   parsley
whole black peppercorns

The best recipe for this traditional dish, usually found along the border country of east Wales, is in *Good Cookery* (1867) by Lady Llanover. The duck is salted, i.e. rubbed and re-rubbed with a ¼ lb of coarse sea salt and, turned for three days while kept in a cool place. The salt is then washed off, and Lady Llanover recommends cooking it in a 'double'—one pan inside another holding water, a *bain marie* in fact. The resulting silky texture of the flesh is incomparable to simply simmering the duck in water. I like to add onion, bay leaf, parsley and black peppercorns. This very gentle cooking will take about 2 hours depending on the age of the duck. All the fat will have been carried off in the water—an excellent stock for lentil soup. Serve either cold or hot—the former is best, but if the latter, a simple onion sauce goes well with it and is traditional.

onion sauce: Cut up 4 onions and stew in a 'double' with a little water until tender, pour off the water, mix it with ½ oz flour, add ½ pint milk, stir till smooth. Press through a wire sieve (or liquidise), return to the double saucepan, stir well while heating through.